Disability and Transition to Adulthood

Achieving independent living

The Joseph Rowntree Foundation has supported this project as part of its programme of research and innovative development projects, which it hopes will be of value to policy makers and practitioners. The facts presented and the views expressed in this report, however, are those of the authors and not necessarily those of the Foundation.

Contents

Acknowledgements

The authors are deeply indebted to the young disabled adults who let us into their lives, allowed us to tape-record interviews and helped us to find our sample. Without their support and enthusiasm this research could not have taken place.

We are also very grateful to the many individuals and organisations who generously gave us time, knowledge and contacts. This includes members of the advisory group, administrative staff and other colleagues at Nottingham, as well as the many disability organisations whose help we used and needed. In the interests of confidentiality for our respondents, we have given less full acknowledgement than we would like to some organisations and individuals, but among the many who helped us are:

- Bhariti Crack
- Steven Crosby
- Vanessa Davies
- Shirley Garner
- David Gibbs
- David Giles
- Maureen Green
- John Hawthorn
- Tim Howells
- Jude Jones
- Richard Kendall
- Sue Kennedy
- Ann Kestenbaum
- David Ladipo
- Sue Lees
- Sandy Marshall
- Jenny Morris
- Alison Neal
- Fiona Neuri
- Barbara Norton
- Kate Punter
- Richard Silburn
- Richard Southorn
- Leicestershire and Rutland Guild of Disabled People
- Derbyshire Disabled Youth Project
- Sheffield Forum for People with Disabilities

Our thanks go to Joy Murray, Geoff Murray, George Thorpe, James Wroughton and Yvonne Lindley for driving the researcher to and from interviews nation-wide.

We owe a very special debt to the Joseph Rowntree Foundation, which funded the research, to Charlie Lloyd, our manager and chair of the advisory board, and to Alison Haigh, for her exceptional administrative support.

Nicola Hendey
Gillian Pascall
School of Sociology and Social Policy
University of Nottingham

Chapter One

Introduction

How can young people with significant impairments achieve independent adulthood? And how can social and voluntary services and benefits be modified to enable such young people to grow into adulthood rather than to disable them? Research points to difficulties in achieving adult goals such as employment, and to inadequate support as young people 'hurtle into a void' (Morris, 1999a). But some young adults with significant impairments achieve independent living, and this study centres on these achievements. It asks young people who have employment and independent households, or one of them, what has enabled their transition to independent living as adults.

To be able to live independently is a key target and struggle for people with disabilities. Since the 1970s the independent living movement has been developed by disabled people to represent their right to live as adults with whatever means are needed to live independently in the community. Supporting people with a wide variety of needs in the community rather than in institutions is also a key Government policy.

'Disabled people have a right to support which will enable them to live independently and with dignity.' (DSS, 1998 p9)

Transition to adulthood is more complex in the face of needs for personal assistance, employment difficulties, housing needs and benefit rules (Burchardt, 2000a). Families, schools and other agencies may treat disabled people as children longer because of their physical needs and perceived vulnerability. Current research suggests that disabled children have a high risk of growing up in poverty (Baldwin, 1985; Baldwin & Carlisle, 1994; Gordon & Heslop, 1998; Gordon *et al*, 2000), and achieve adult goals in employment, economic independence, personal autonomy, independent housing and citizenship to a lesser degree and at a later stage than non-disabled adults (Hendey, 1998; Morris, 1999a, 1999b). Disabled young people are less likely than young people in general to live independently of their parents, and half as likely to be in paid work. They are also often not in control of their own financial and social lives (Hirst & Baldwin, 1994). The benefits system has traps for those who need personal assistance and seek independence (Kestenbaum, 1997, 1998, 1999). In previous research on the difficulties of achieving adulthood for this group, we had no single individual who combined paid employment and independent householding (Hendey, 1998). We designed the current project, in deliberate contrast, to seek out young disabled adults with both independent households and paid employment, as well as comparative groups with one or other of these or neither.

The number of young people with complex physical impairments reaching adulthood is growing (Morris, 1999a). The

Government acknowledges that current systems *'do not adequately recognise the greater needs of those disabled early in life'* (DSS, 1998 p1). We have asked respondents about supports in social and voluntary provision and in their families that have enabled their transition to adulthood and which might contribute to policy development.

Adulthood

What has age to do with adulthood? In social policy there is no consistency; adulthood is reached at different ages in different contexts. Social scientists have seen the process of becoming adult as a series of transitions – from school to work, from family of origin to family of destination, from parental home to own home – rather than as a function of chronological age. These transitions also became more extended and problematic towards the end of the twentieth century with unemployment, the transformation of the youth labour market and policy changes that extricated the state from supporting young people. The diversity of young people themselves has increasingly been acknowledged in terms of class, race and gender, and – more rarely – disability. Transition can no longer be seen as a single, idealised pathway built on the white male, able-bodied life-course of the post-war era (Coles, 1995; Jones, 1995; Jones & Bell, 2000). The evidence that young disabled people reach such goals – if they reach them at all – later than their peers extends our notion of transition.

Paid employment has often been seen as the key transition to adulthood, both in itself and as a key to other transitions of householding, partnering and parenting, adult social relations and citizenship. Current Government policy emphasises meeting the obligations of citizenship through paid work.

The disability movement, as well as the sociological literature, has questioned the status of paid employment as the key criterion of adulthood. People with impairments are deeply disadvantaged in the labour market, less likely than their peers to be employed, much less likely to be in good jobs with high earnings. If society and social policy assume paid work as the key to independent adulthood, those who do not achieve it may be treated as children. But if young disabled people have the same aspirations as their peers, paid employment will be among their ambitions. The evidence also points to paid work as the most likely route away from poverty and into full membership of a consumer society. This poses dilemmas for young disabled people as well as for policy.

We have used paid employment as a practical criterion for selecting our sample of independent adults. But we keep the relative significance of jobs, householding, social relations, citizenship and financial independence as subjects for our respondents. Do our respondents share the priority the Government gives to paid employment as the key to independence as adults? How does it relate to these other aspects of adulthood? Some respondents described friends and social networks. Some described intimate relationships and parenthood. But more described the difficulty of all these. The literature suggests that, while young people in general have extending social horizons as they get older, young disabled people may be more narrowly confined within home and family (Hirst & Baldwin, 1994). It is possible as a young disabled adult to lead a 'madcap sort of a life' (Hendey, 1998), with the kind of spontaneity and social interaction that most young adults take for granted. But this was not the general experience of our respondents. Those with jobs and their own households were more likely to have some of the basics: income, personal assistance, transport and social networks from their jobs.

Independence is another problematic concept. Interdependence is a much better way to describe how most of us actually live. We are all dependent as children and risk dependence in old age. In between – even in an individualistic society – we may carry out personal tasks for each other, depend on one another for sharing income, household resources and services, and on structures beyond the household for income, employment, housing, health and education. So does it make sense to see the main dynamic of adulthood as the transition from dependence to independence (Tisdall, 2000)? But independence is the concept used by the disability movement in the demand for independent living. Centres for Independent Living have expressed their demands as access to appropriate housing, personal assistance, transport, access to their environment, advocacy and training, information and counselling and equipment or technical assistance (Hendey, 1998). These demands are about putting the means at the disposal of disabled people to take control of their own lives, rather than about a particular vision of independent adulthood; the demands notably exclude paid employment, for example. In keeping the notion of independence, we are not supposing that any adults are wholly independent, or prejudging the form that independence may take. In particular, we acknowledge that an idealised notion of independent adulthood is a normative construction which is *'not only disabling, but highly gendered and ethnocentric'* (Priestley, 2000a p426; 2001b).

The research

Using snowball sampling, seventy-two young adults were interviewed from four groups.

Our 'most independent' respondents were 31 young adults living independently and in employment (group 1). We had three smaller comparative groups: two 'less independent', who had either independent living (17 respondents, group 2) or employment (12 respondents, group 3), and one 'least independent' group (12 respondents, group 4), who were living with parents and unemployed. To focus on growing up with disability, we selected respondents impaired from birth or early childhood. All received the care component of Disability Living Allowance (DLA), which was a key criterion for inclusion in the sample. This benefit is designed to help with extra disability-related costs and is awarded at different rates on the basis of care and mobility needs. Thirty-two respondents were receiving the care component at the higher rate and thirty-one at the middle rate. Following advice during the research, we added respondents with learning impairments and with sensory impairments.

To talk about the transition to adulthood with young disabled people who had accomplished it, we were obliged to extend our age range beyond the early twenties. This decision is supported by the evidence of the key quantitative study of young people with disabilities by Hirst and Baldwin (1994), though it leads to a more extended age range than in their study and most others, from 21 to 35 years old, with 41 respondents in their twenties and 31 in their early thirties. Eight respondents were from ethnic minorities. There were 32 male respondents and 40 female. Seven respondents had learning difficulties.

We intended to draw comparative samples which were broadly equivalent in terms of age, gender, ethnicity and levels of impairment. In the event, there was little difference in age between the sample groups (*Figure 1*, below), but men were over-represented among the 'most independent'

Figure 1 Age by householding/employment group

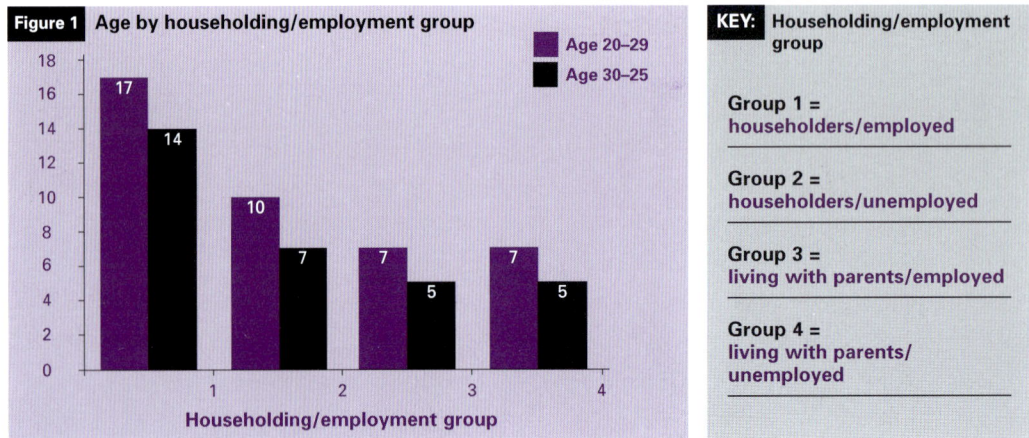

KEY: Householding/employment group

Group 1 = householders/employed

Group 2 = householders/unemployed

Group 3 = living with parents/employed

Group 4 = living with parents/ unemployed

group (*Figure 2*, below), as were ethnic minorities. There were proportionately rather more recipients of the highest care benefits among the independent living/unemployed group (14 out of 17), while each of the other three groups had one-third in this highest category (*Figure 3*, opposite). It should be borne in mind that this comparative group, living independently/unemployed, have a higher level of impairment and associated care need than the others. None of these differences can be interpreted in terms of statistical significance because the samples were not drawn randomly, but we discuss their implications at appropriate points in the text.

We had ten respondents with the highest care benefits who were also in jobs and living independently. Some respondents had full lives as adults, with jobs, households, social lives and a sense of equality as citizens. They show the possibility. But, despite our vigorous pursuit, such respondents were rare. Few described spontaneous and rich social lives and few felt themselves to be equal citizens with non-disabled peers. Very few had well-paid jobs, established careers or independent housing of their choice. We found no respondents with learning disabilities who were both living independently and employed.

Figure 2 Gender by householding/employment group

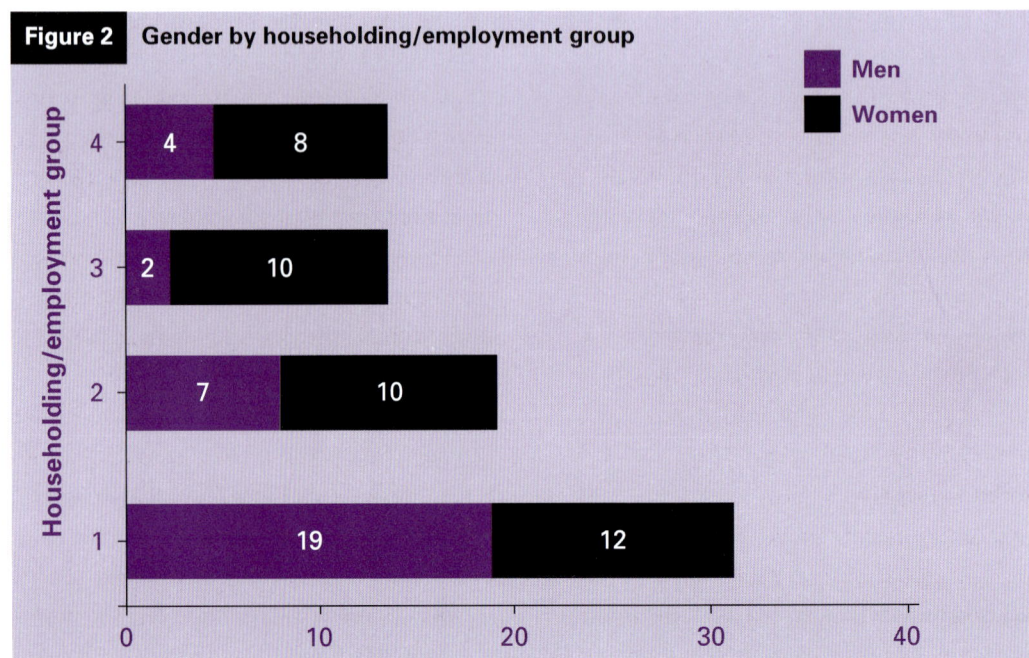

Figure 3 DLA entitlement by householding/employment group

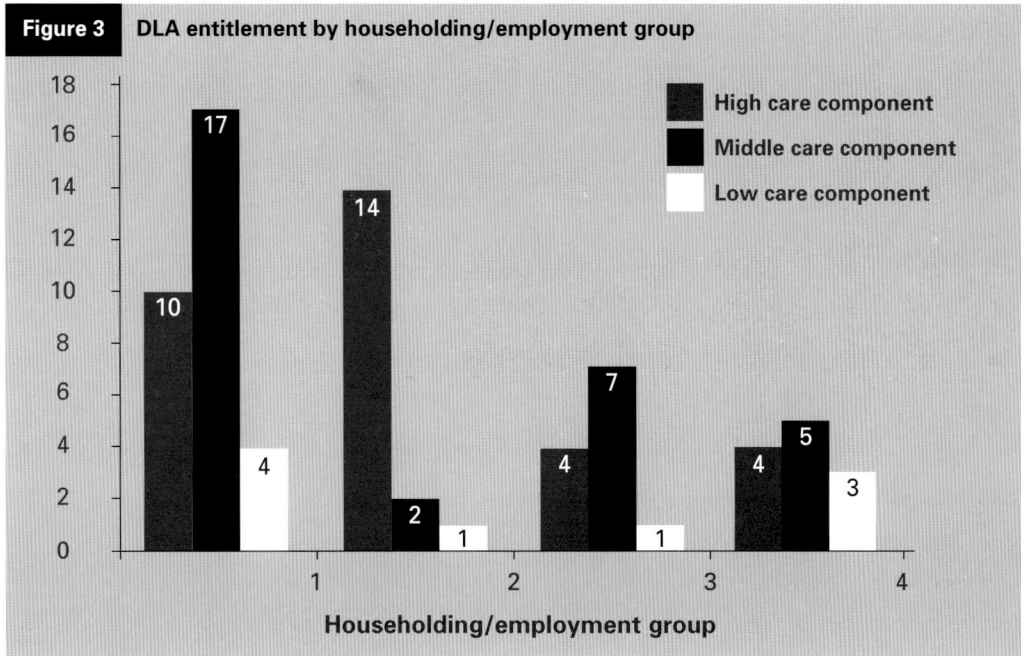

Legend:
- High care component
- Middle care component
- Low care component

Values: Group 1: 10, 17, 4 / Group 1 (second): 14, 2, 1 / Group 2: 4, 7, 1 / Group 3: 4, 5, 3

X-axis: Householding/employment group

We approached a wide range of employers, beginning with disability organisations; we asked major companies and banks, an organisation of disabled professionals, social service departments and specialist teams and a major specialist housing project. Everywhere we met enthusiasm for the project and scepticism about locating suitable individuals. Employers tended to find that their disabled employees had not grown up with impairments. But most approaches brought someone to the sample. We used a number of information services: the CanDo Web site, a national information service based at Lancaster University careers service, an article in *Occupational Therapy Weekly*. One participant set up a web page for the project and posted details on disability websites. Respondents were more widely dispersed than we had intended, mainly from the Midlands, but also North Yorkshire, London and Wales.

The research methods aimed to get as close to the ideals of emancipatory research as possible. Qualitative research was used with semi-structured in-depth interviews. Pseudonyms were introduced at the beginning of the interviews and used throughout the research; the report uses these and, on occasion, a double pseudonym to protect identities. Disabled people were consulted at all stages of the research. An exception was made in the case of learning-disabled respondents, whose parents were usually interviewed. This resulted in rather different data which has been difficult to accommodate in the report as fully as we would like, and we acknowledge that the methodology for accessing this group of respondents should be tailored more specifically to this purpose from the outset (Grove *et al*, 2000).

The report examines key structures which may support transition to adulthood, starting with families and moving on to wider social structures such as education, housing, work and benefit provisions. Each chapter highlights the respondents who had achieved paid employment and independent living, drawing comparisons with the others as appropriate.

Chapter Two
Parents

Our respondents grew up towards the end of the twentieth century, when the dominant ideology was that state responsibility for children risked undermining parental responsibility. The policies flowing from these ideas, combined with an economic policy of containing public expenditure, put responsibilities on families. Child Benefit levels were checked. State support for childcare was resisted, despite women's increasing labour market participation. More was demanded of families in supporting young people, as the youth labour market collapsed and benefits to young adults were reduced. While young people in general responded by leaving home earlier than ever, deeming independence more important than the risks (Jones, 1995), young people with impairments found leaving home very difficult (Hendey, 1998), perhaps more so in the case of those with learning difficulties (Riddell, 1998). How could they become independent of their parents?

Parents were most often seen by our most independent respondents as the source of their ability to achieve independent adulthood. The chapter therefore starts with the qualities these most independent respondents saw in their parents, in terms of independent living, expectations, resources, and ability to negotiate with professionals, before offering the accounts of the comparative groups.

Parents and independent living

Our most independent respondents, when asked what factor most helped them to become independent, talked most of *'parental encouragement'* (Ann), *'having the support of the family behind me 110% in whatever I've done'* (Paul), *'confidence that has come from the support of the family'* (Tim). Some specified maternal support: *'living in a one-parent family, my mum has been very supportive'* (Tim).

What did these respondents value in their parents? A combination of nurture/protection with fostering of independence was one feature. Ann described parents whose care was hard-edged.

> *'When it came to teaching me to even put my socks or my shoes on and whatever, I was left for an hour to struggle... I know it sounds cruel... sometimes I ended up being able to do it in an hour or so and sometimes I didn't, but if I didn't, then it would get done for me, but then the next week or day or whatever I'd be given another shot.'*

Ann explained her current level of independence – doing without personal assistance – in terms of the practice and attitude of mind engendered by these parental strategies.

Rachel describes a similar experience.

'*My mum… would sort of push me into going out and about and making my own life really… if picking a cup up "you can do it yourself, do it yourself", not "let me do it for you"… She's never been one for sort of mollycoddling and mothering… it's bordering on the hard really, it must've been hard for her to watch me struggle and seeing me sort of fail… but it's the best thing she ever did.*'

The balancing of nurture with strategies to foster independence was clearly difficult. The rarity of such parenting was acknowledged by respondents.

'*I haven't had the babying that other people have had… my parents have always expected me to get on with it.*' (Jane)

Expectations

Parental expectations also figured large in these accounts, often in contrast with the expectations of others, especially of professionals. John's mother…

'*…expected me* (John) *to do and have exactly the same things that everybody else was expected to have*'.

Ann described parents who…

'*…were a lot more confident of what they thought I* (Ann) *would be capable of than what you could call experts*'.

From Kate's parents came implicit confidence.

'*It was almost an unspoken thing, it was just that I* (Kate) *was expected to succeed… a lot was expected of me and I expected a lot from myself.*'

Expectations about educational achievement were high.

'*I felt a lot of pressure on me to do well academically.*' (Kate)

Rachel's mum…

'*…was all for me* (Rachel) *going out and making a life… not so much pushing to get a job… but to college and then they wanted me to go to university although at the time I didn't want to*'.

Work was also an expectation from John's parents who…

'*…never made me* (John) *feel that I could use being disabled as some kind of excuse for not working*'.

Matthew's father…

'*…kept on saying it to me* (Matthew)… *it became rather boring… but he was right… as long as you know what you want to do… especially with your disability, you need to know what you want to do from an early age*'.

Kate's account of her parents' attitudes about living independently was…

'*…there was just no way that I* (Kate) *could have carried on living at home because they just knew that I was capable of not living at home… it was almost unspoken really, just the expectation that I would get out and get on with my own life*'.

Richard's parents had always…

'*…encouraged me* (Richard) *to move on and that sort of included leaving home*'.

These respondents described parents whose expectations were that they would become adult like any other, with education, employment and homes of their own, and would look after themselves.

Resources

Our most independent respondents also described parents' material, cultural and social support starting in the nursery and continuing in adulthood. Behind these accounts there often lurks awareness of the limitations of other resources, of other young people who had much worse experiences, and of alternatives escaped.

> *'My parents have always pushed me. I could read and write before I started nursery, which was down to my mum… a lot of the children in the unit didn't leave with any GCSEs… as it was, I left with nine.'* (Jane)

Support for moving out was often active, practical and concrete. John's parents had provided a loan for a deposit on a house and help with finding it.

> *'We couldn't possibly have moved here unless we could have looked at getting a mortgage… the reason why we've got this place is because of John's mother's good work in finding it for us.'* (Kathy)

For Paul, information about housing was crucial and…

> *'…the only way I (Paul) would have known about that is through Mum'.*

Kate's mother's career advice was to…

> *'…use the fact that I (Kate) had the identity of a disabled person to try and see if it could open up things for me rather than close it off'.*

Toby's family helped in finding a job.

While these respondents valued their independence, they acknowledged their parents' continuing moral and practical support. Richard's parents were…

> *'…helping me (Richard) to establish myself in my own home, and if I needed anything they would still be there, if I needed any assistance with anything I couldn't do myself'.*

Kate's parents still…

> *'…sort me (Kate) out if I've had a fall or they'll always make sure I'm OK despite being now at an age and a level now where they're not fighting my battles for me'.*

Respondents from the comparative groups made much less reference to material support from their parents. Analysis of parental occupations (ONS, 2000) shows more with higher occupational categories (1–4) in both independent living groups, and more with lower occupational categories (5–8) in both groups living with parents (***Figure 4***, below).

Parents and professionals

The ability to negotiate with professionals – and to oppose them when necessary – was another feature (Beresford, 1994, 2000; Thomas, 1998 p94; Read, 2000).

Experience with an older sibling had taught Kate's parents to challenge medical assumptions.

Figure 4 Parental occupation by independent householding/employment group

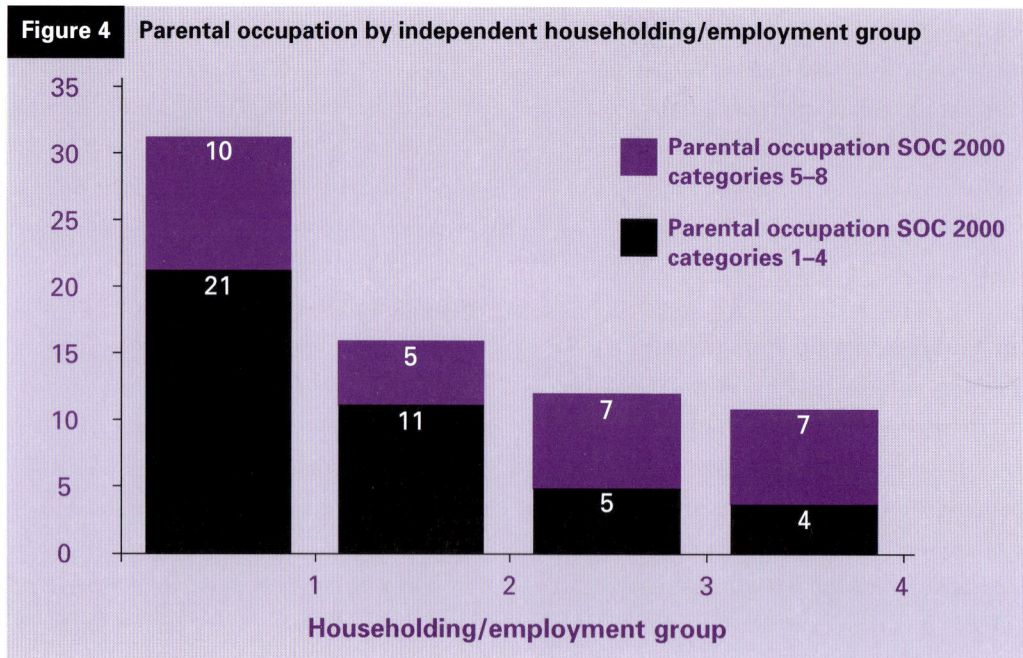

'She was symptomatic before I was and she
was always the one that first of all had all
the attention, all the prodding and poking
from doctors and this, that and the other
and experimental "let's see if this helps".'

Education could also be a battle-ground.

'The doctors told them that they'd never get
me past primary school... well, they fought
to send me to a mainstream school.' (Lucy)

Ann's parents faced a range of professionals.

'There was the teachers at the special
school, then there was the school nurse,
and the school doctor as well said that
I wouldn't cope and I think they got quite
nasty at one point.'

Our most independent respondents
described a style of parenting that fitted them
for independent living in an individualistic
world. They were never allowed to think
they might not be capable of academic
achievement, of keeping a job or living

independently. The social model of disability
demands a level of recognition and support
for the needs resulting from physical
impairment which is at present far from
realisation. Individuals with significant
impairments needed to rely on their own and
their families' resources. These respondents
gave accounts of parents who cared, fought
and negotiated for them, but also ensured
that they could care, fight and negotiate for
themselves. They were, in general, relatively
privileged parents in educational and
economic terms.

Close relations

Respondents in the less and least
independent groups often described equally
warm and close relations with their parents,
without the astringent edge that our most
independent respondents identified as
propelling them to independent adulthood.
Alice's account of her parents described their
enabling and permissive support.

'I couldn't want for better parents for being supportive or anything like that… They've been "you can get whatever job you want if that's what you want to do or you don't have to get a job if you don't want".'

Sarah too spoke of close family support.

'We've always been there for each other, in fact, the whole family is there for each other, if we need.'

But the closeness of family relationships could hinder independent living. Earlier research has shown the risk that young disabled adults will have diminishing social worlds, while their able-bodied peers are establishing wider networks (Hirst & Baldwin, 1994). Steve described family bonds as a barrier which he did not feel ready to climb over.

'With disabled people, those bonds are a lot stronger, and so it takes a lot more effort… it's very, very difficult indeed.'

Peter, in the absence of wider social relationships, relied on his mother for emotional support and guidance.

'I always go back to my mum to explain, like talk to her with any problems or anything like that.'

Respondents were often aware that their parents relied on them.

'My mum… I think I am her life and she's told me that I am before… My mum would miss me if I left home because she would have nobody to look after.' (Alice)

These parents also appeared to have fewer economic, cultural and social resources to pass on to their children.

Difficult relations

Some respondents living with parents appeared very accepting of their situation, especially where they had nursing needs. Others had made vigorous attempts to move out, sometimes with parental support, but were hampered by housing or care problems.

Tracey described family relationships as damaging.

'They find me difficult to live with, the reality of having a disabled member of the family… They keep implying… that I'm stupid, I never do anything for myself… all I do is cause work for them… I feel very unloved.'

Social divisions

Leaving home may have presented more difficulties to our young women respondents than to the men; women were over-represented in both comparative groups living with parents. The difficulty of earning enough to cover costs would have been greater for women respondents in general. Among ethnic minority respondents, other issues were raised. Some described parents with low expectations of them as daughters, as impaired, and as future workers or partners. In this case teachers and social workers had sometimes provided key support for achieving independence. Young women met some opposition to their plans for marriage or cohabitation.

'My dad didn't want me to move out because I was going to be living with somebody else, living with another man.' (Chanda)

Young disabled women might be supporting parents as interpreters and negotiators with the outside world.

*'They don't want to be left on their own...
they depend on me an awful lot.'* (Meena)

Becoming parents

Marriage and parenthood were rare among
our respondents. Some respondents spoke
of partnerships which supported their
independence. John and Kathy felt they
succeeded better as a disabled couple than
either could have done separately.

> *'Jointly... we consider ourselves that
> we're reaching a point where we are
> contributing to society more than we
> are taking from... separately, I think
> we probably still would have been
> swallowing up resources.'*

But the difficulties of making relationships
figured larger, especially the difficulties of
feeling attractive to others. Diane found it
hard to think to herself...

> *'...yes, I am attractive and yes, someone
> would want to be with me just for me...
> I think that's a real big issue.'.*

Being a parent was even rarer. Responsibility
for others brought new issues. Hard-won
independence as an individual felt
compromised for David by his children's
needs. He accepted help from friends to take
them out.

> *'It's hard to be independent if you've got
> kids and you don't drive.'* (David)

Parenthood raised issues of dependency,
especially acutely. Nicky talked of giving up
a baby.

> *'I don't think it would have been fair
> on her... seeing me needing lots of help
> as well.'*

Conclusion

Parents were our respondents' most
important resource. Disability fosters close
relationships between parents and children,
with care unshared (Glendinning, 1983).
Parents may attend to children for longer,
offer skilled nursing care and support them
with domestic crises. Exceptional parents
with exceptional resources may also underpin
the transition to independent living as
adults. Our most independent respondents
described a hard-edged care that fostered
independence. But these parents also had a
relatively high level of social, economic and
cultural resources in comparison with the
others. Most parents, most of the time, with
fewer advantages of their own, will find this
impossible. Our comparative respondents
described a style of parenting less concerned
with fostering their independence. They also
gave less evidence of parents who had
cultural, social and material resources.

Policies which have increasingly turned
to parents to support their children have
opened a void between family support and
independent living which is hard to cross.
Our least independent respondents could feel
trapped in parental homes; it could be very
difficult to grow away from the very close
relationships that disability fostered. The lack
of supports beyond the family presented
some respondents with an impassable barrier
to independent adulthood. Young disabled
people need, like others, to move beyond
their families of origin, and they need support
to meet needs with personal care, nursing,
housing, income and jobs if they are to grow
to independent adulthood.

Few of our respondents had moved
through being parented to being parents
themselves.

Chapter Three
Education

Inclusion has been official policy since the 1944 *Education Act*. The disability movement has seen exclusion into segregated institutions as a violation of human rights; '*remediation, care and control were the primary functions of these institutions*' (Armstrong & Barton, 1999). But segregation has been a continuing reality for disabled children often, in practice, excluded from mainstream education. Mainstream schooling has begun to adopt the social model of disability with (rather weak) requirements under the *Disability Discrimination Act* for anti-discriminatory policies (Gooding, 1996, 2000; Robinson & Stalker, 1998; Leicester, 1999; Drake, 1999, 2000; Cooper, 2000). The Tomlinson Report on further education asks for inclusion rather than integration, to change the educational environment to enable young people with impairments to participate fully via the '*redesign of the very processes of learning, assessment and organisation so as to fit the objectives and learning styles of students*' (Tomlinson, 1996 p4). This moves beyond giving students with impairments additional human or physical aids to gain access to courses. But what is our respondents' experience of education systems? Of segregation? And how well is mainstream education responding to children with impairments, including them and supporting their needs?

We also need to ask about the mainstream education marketplace and the power of parents of disabled children. Parental choice may enable parents to achieve appropriate schooling for their disabled children. But the 1988 *Education (Reform) Act*, with its emphasis on league tables, local management, increasing selection and opting out of local education authority control, makes it harder for schools to accept disabled children. The *Disability Discrimination Act* offers only conditional access to mainstream schools (Kenworthy & Whittaker, 2000; Murray, 2000). Are the choices of parents with disabled children especially restricted? And, in a diversifying marketplace, are their children being left with ever poorer places in or out of mainstream schools?

Educational achievements

The importance of education to young people's achievement of jobs and independent living will scarcely be a surprise. The majority of the most independent group had a minimum of five O levels/GCSEs (or equivalent) at grades A–C. Half had degrees and two had postgraduate qualifications. None had a learning impairment. These respondents spoke of schools with high academic expectations, full access to the curriculum and good support in the classroom, whether segregated or mainstream. John's mainstream school was…

> '…*keen for me* (John) *to do the best work that I could. We were very positively integrated.*'.

Ian's segregated school for the visually impaired was…

> '…highly geared in all areas… there was a tremendous amount of pressure. You almost had to go to college or university'.

The staff at Tom's segregated school *'pushed you all the time'*, while Richard's segregated school for the visually impaired gave…

> '…the best possible education they could of any school of its kind. I (Richard) was able to do a good range of subjects up to O and A level'.

Lucy at mainstream school had a carer to scribe for her, and Jo had full subject choice.

> 'There was a slight fear of me doing drama because I think they thought that I might hold the class back, but we had two drama teachers who were great and they pushed for me to do it.'

But such educational achievement among young disabled adults is rare, and the experience of the comparative groups was in sharp contrast. These respondents themselves were quite varied, some in work and some out, some on the way to independent living, while others seemed likely to live in the parental home for a long time yet. But of all these 36 respondents without learning impairments, seven had five GCSEs at Grades A to C, one of whom had a degree. Eleven had not been entered for any examinations. Most spoke of low expectations framed by their impairments rather than their abilities, poor diagnosis of their problems, limited opportunities and low educational standards. Frank described limited opportunities.

> 'The school gave me fewer opportunities because they thought I had a reading difficulty, which I didn't.'

Indeira attributed her high achievements to her parents rather than to her school.

> 'Because the teaching quality was not of such a good standard I don't think we got the best push to achieve. I was lucky in terms of my family. My parents pushed me to achieve what I have.'

Our most independent respondents described positive educational experiences, in academically-oriented segregated schools or in well-integrated mainstream ones. They were highly qualified. They would find the labour market hostile, but at least they had the resources to enter it. The picture drawn by all the comparative groups was of low expectations; most achieved nothing that would give them access to a demanding labour market. The comparative groups also showed the other side of the coin of segregated schooling – their poor experiences were mainly of segregated schools.

Segregated and mainstream schools

When we focus on the issue of mainstream against segregated schooling, the picture is complex. The majority of respondents overall – 44 out of 72 – had been to segregated schools. But their accounts did not fit neatly into the pattern set for them by the disability movement. Several respondents spoke very positively of segregated schools with a strong academic orientation and thought mainstream would have been worse. However, most of these were schools for the visually impaired; one catered for people with mobility impairments.

Respondents drew attention to the skilled specialist teaching, accessibility of the curriculum, schools with resources for small-group teaching and the peer group support that they had experienced in these segregated schools. David commented that…

'…all of the teachers in the school were qualified not just in their subject but in teaching blind people how to do their subject'.

At Nigel's school for people with mobility impairments…

'…being there, you were exposed to people from various backgrounds, given various opportunities to explore pursuits, gain qualifications. I don't believe that I would have left mainstream school with that level of knowledge'.

Ian thought he would have done worse in a comprehensive school. He said, *'the fact that we were in very small classes was very important'* in his school for the visually impaired.

David summed up the advantages while adding the social limitations.

'Specialist education is generally the way to go, because mainly you have got the staff who know how to teach blind people and you have got stuff in accessible format and you have other blind people around which does help psychologically… because sighted people just work faster, which is really, really frustrating because you have the brain to do it but it is just faster for a sighted person. I know it's not very politically correct, but that is just the way it is. It is so demoralising if you are slower. You tend to get a better education but a worse social environment.'

Other respondents, with different experiences, picked up the social disadvantages more strongly.

'I would much rather see disabled people go through mainstream education because in my opinion it's a better way to go. You give

as good as you get. The teachers will give you the help when you ask for it, but they know that it is not just you that needs the help, it is 25 other people in the class. They need the help but in a different way. I would much rather go through mainstream school, as segregated school is more one-to-one and that is not what I wanted. I preferred to be helped on a much leveller playing field. They took me for what I was – a regular human being.' (Paul)

The trend towards inclusion in mainstream education has strong support from the disability movement and is likely to continue. But respondents who had attended the best segregated schools remind us that there can be losses from integration as well as gains, especially in the specialist teaching skills and more generous levels of support.

Segregation was the typical experience of the comparative respondents, though there was a small majority of the living with parents / employed group – 7 out of 12 – who had attended mainstream (*Figure 5*, overleaf). Jodie's account of segregation was of misdiagnosis, low expectations and poor classroom support, based on the assumption that she had a profound learning disability.

'My mum has been telling the school that I'm dyslexic and they never did anything. They said that I'd got a learning disability. I didn't have enough help in the classroom because the expectations weren't there so it didn't matter kind of thing.'

So, while some segregated schools were described as places with academic orientation, high expectations, quality teaching and achievements, most segregated schools were perceived by their students as adding to their disabilities. This experience of schooling and achievement is more typical of the experience of disabled children in general.

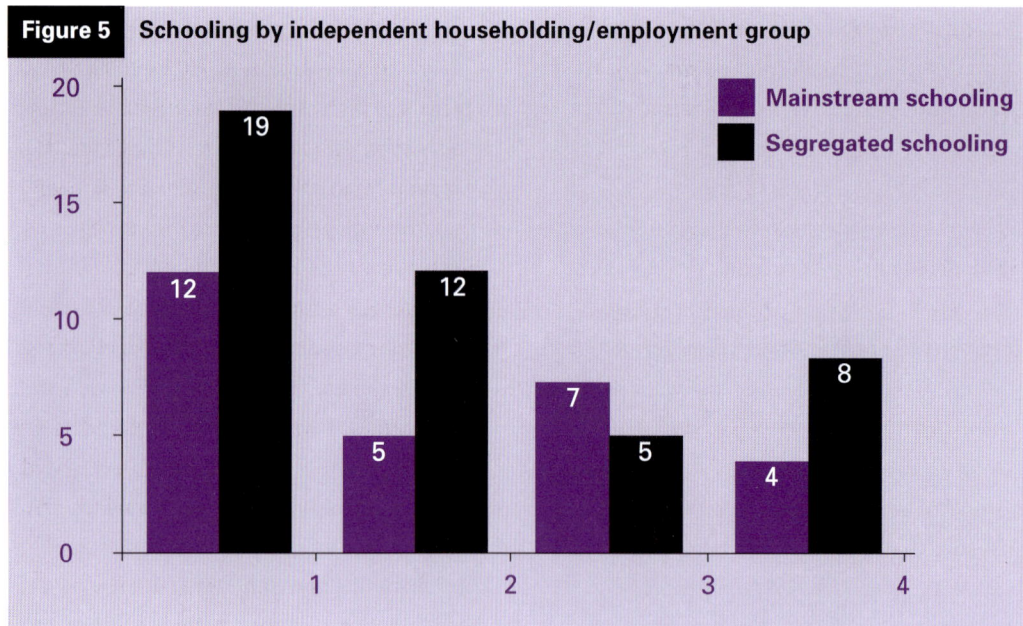

Figure 5 Schooling by independent householding/employment group

Segregation in itself brings problems. As Paul remarked, above, it is difficult to become *'a regular human being'* in an environment built around impairment. Segregation may also risk creating damaging environments, outweighing the benefits of specialist skills.

Accessing education

Access to the curriculum, to schools, and to education itself is not something disabled children can take for granted.

Even our most independent respondents remind us of the risk of educational exclusion that disabled children carry. Many spoke of individual advocates who had won education for them, rather than of supportive educational structures. Ann's parents had fought for her access to mainstream schooling. Saul's teacher insisted on his abilities.

'I was quite intelligent but lucky at the same time. The most important break that I had was a teacher who insisted that I was clever enough to go to comprehensive. She gave me an IQ test and held the results up to the school and said to them "you have to take him" so they had no choice.'

Education policy favours access to education through inclusion within the mainstream, but the experience of our respondents was that it was only won by advocacy and in competition.

Respondents in the comparative groups help us to understand the limitations of schooling for children with impairments, as well as the depth of the disability movement's rejection of segregated schooling – for many of these respondents, segregation meant denial of education itself.

Respondents with learning difficulties rarely had adequate support for accessing education, especially where they had a combination of impairments, learning, visual and/or mobility.

Social divisions

Respondents from ethnic minorities who were also visually impaired described difficulties because their language needs were not fully supported, especially when they also had visual impairment. Sally came to England in childhood, when she also lost her eyesight.

'I was put into mainstream school and was expected to compete the same as everybody else... I had problems with English... I just found it very, very difficult and very stressful.'

For Meena, who described her parents as unsupportive, it was teachers who enabled her to become more independent.

'I think it was the teachers really... I got a lot of guidance, not from school but from college.'

Conclusion

Our most independent respondents spoke warmly of both segregated schools with specialist skills and mainstream schools which integrated them. They emerged with qualifications. Other groups of respondents, speaking mainly of segregated schools, described low expectations and low achievements which left them very poorly equipped for a transforming labour market.

How can we interpret the very different experience of segregated education among our respondents with jobs and independent households and the others? The marketplace for segregated schools has been very diverse, with a few academically-oriented schools winning high achievements and loyalty from our respondents, while the majority experience of segregation is of exclusion from educational achievement. Limited access to quality schools has put parents of disabled children into intense competition with each other, a competition likely to be won by the most economically and culturally advantaged. The disability movement and the policy environment are likely to continue the move towards mainstream education, preferring its inclusive possibilities and aware of the damage done by the poorer segregated schools. But disabled children in mainstream environments do not thrive without the specialist skills and more intensive support that have characterised the better segregated schools. They need to be rescued and developed for disabled children in all educational environments.

If this educational marketplace has been behind the very varied responses to segregation among our respondents, we should also ask about the chances of disabled children in an increasingly market-driven education system. Markets are a centrifugal force in mainstream education, too, and parents may have to fight ever harder to achieve appropriate schools for their disabled children. They need stronger defence than the *Disability Discrimination Act* to support their access to appropriate schools and their position within them.

Chapter Four
Housing

The independent living movement demands inclusion and citizenship. In housing terms this should mean greater accessibility/adaptability for all housing: the concept of lifetime homes in contrast with that of special needs (Lewis, 1993). Those fighting for more inclusive housing standards have recently achieved some success. New regulations will make new housing more accessible and contribute to a more inclusive housing environment (Bull, 2000). But current access standards in the general housing stock are very low and very divisive. The drift of housing policy affecting our respondents over the 1980s and 1990s has produced diverging paths. Increasingly, for the general population, being a householder means being an owner occupier. The privileged status of owner occupation has been widely extended. But access standards are generally low and costs may be high; both can exclude disabled people. Disabled people have had their 'special needs' met by housing associations with accessible social housing (Stewart *et al*, 1999). This can produce physical segregation in separate housing schemes. It can also produce economic segregation. Rising rents for social housing, subsidies transferred from houses to individuals, payment through means-tested Housing Benefit – all these hinder access to work. How do young disabled adults negotiate access to independent housing, with what support and at what cost?

Working for owner occupation

Half of our most independent group of respondents (and one other) were owner occupiers, with at least some of the choice and control over suitability that this usually implies, and its claim to a wider citizenship.

Sylvia – exceptionally – had resources from a medical negligence case which funded her housing and personal assistance. She was able to put her housing in place before starting training for her career.

'The adaptations and things were being done during my final year at university so that when I came to start my work training I moved in just before that.'

A few respondents had help from housing associations to establish themselves in owner occupation, through joint ownership or deposit schemes.

'The housing association that I was at previous to this – they offered several thousand for me to actually move out of that flat, so I put that into a deposit and had the rest as a mortgage… it worked out well.' (Will)

Among respondents with jobs, the difficulties in accessing fit housing, let alone housing that enabled a full adult life, dominated the accounts. Kate felt that *'the lack of choice is just stunning'*. Respondents described great difficulties in reaching the position where they had suitable accessible housing. John's difficulties were…

> '*…enhanced because he just cannot fit into any temporary accommodation*'. (Kathy)

Job mobility was another serious issue. Kate had moved to a new job with a month's notice to find somewhere suitable. She would prefer to live where there was '*a little bit going on*', but was living out of town in a privately rented bungalow and employing personal assistants to take her wheelchair in and out…

> '*…because my* (Kate's) *house is inaccessible… the bathroom isn't accessible and it's not only a problem for me personally – it's a problem because I happen to know lots of people who also need their access needs to be met… my sister can't come to stay here, quite a lot of my friends can't go to the toilet… Not being able to find accessible places to live and not being able to find accessible places to work – they've been the two main things that have held me back*'. (Kate)

The costs of accessible accommodation were a major problem for respondents with jobs. Dan had to rent.

> '*I could live somewhere smaller… if I wasn't in a wheelchair, but the fact is I need a bungalow and a lot of space so I wouldn't be able to afford a place that would accommodate my requirements.*' (Dan)

Fran – with a job but still living at home – described a series of frustrations: unsuitable local authority offers, rejecting a perfect local authority bungalow which she could not afford from her earnings. She now had a mortgage offer and was looking for somewhere to buy, but was daunted by the amount of work that would be needed.

> '*This brand-new flat would have had to have been turned virtually upside down.*'

Social housing: 'special' housing for 'special' needs

Transition to independent living was addressed in housing association schemes which combined housing and personal assistance and which were generally warmly described by respondents. For Richard, this meant a small rented flat, not too expensive and…

> '*…any sort of maintenance problem, I can call them and they'll come to sort it out*'.

For Toby too a housing association project provided valued support with helpful wardens in a '*really nice community*'.

Some of our most independent respondents had accessed social housing with which they were at least reasonably content. Ann felt lucky renting accessible accommodation through her local authority, knowing its rarity.

> '*I consider myself very lucky to have got that, because I did envisage myself being in a ground-floor one-bedroomed flat, whereas this has got two bedrooms, but I only got it because my orthopaedic surgeon put in a report… the actual adapted accommodation is very limited, you can't decide the sort of area you want to live in.*'

Local authorities resolved some problems, but they did not always give priority to respondents' needs for independence.

> '*I found it very difficult to access any suitable accommodation… It was very difficult for the housing office to accept that persons wanting to become*

independent were worthy of any point priority… We eventually got the offer of a one-bedroom pokey flat, in a run-down area… they said that they wouldn't put a shower in for me and if I wanted access to a shower maybe I should go back to my parents each day and use the shower there.' (Mike)

Mike was eventually able to buy, with his partner.

Respondents without jobs gave more positive accounts of access to social housing. For most of those living independently, housing associations had provided accessible bricks and mortar, offered useful support and a standard of service. Benefits paid the rent. There was one very frustrated account of administrative obstacles, from Owen's parents, of a nine-month wait for adaptations and sanction for a care package. But more often housing associations, occupational therapists and social workers were described warmly.

Mark was living at home when his mother's death precipitated a crisis, and sensitive and efficient services enabled him to become established independently.

'You've got the support of social services in this particular property, because it's a conjunction of the two organisations, the housing association and the social services.'

Tania's occupational therapist *'got the flat for me… she's been very good about adaptations'* and her housing association was *'ever so helpful'* about adaptations. Zoe's support came through social services.

'The social worker… she brought information about housing, housing associations as well… it so happened they were just building these… it's beautiful.'

Ben contrasted his experience in different authorities, but in his current area…

'I (Ben) was consulted on day one, before this was even built… what I needed inside the house, and housing services supported me throughout the whole stage, from applying, to adaptations before I moved in and support after when I needed it.'

He was glad to have some responsibilities taken from him. *'Life is complicated enough anyway'*.

Integration/segregation

Integration with the wider community rather than segregated housing was generally preferred by those who could exercise choice, and by some who could not. Matthew's warm account of a specialised housing scheme for disabled people did not amount to preferring it above any alternative.

'This is housing association. I came here because of the care mainly. In an ideal world I would like to buy my own house but that is not possible because of the care.'

Ian, a teacher, had chosen privately rented accommodation where he was able to lead a full life including his choice of church and friends.

'I love this area… I do feel secure here, yes, there is a community spirit, people speak to you here.'

Dan articulated his need for housing that reflected his personality rather than his impairment, and his need to be part of a wider community than that of disabled people.

'I don't want to live where disabled people live. I want to live where I want to live because of who I am, not because I'm different… I want to be treated the same as everybody else.'

For people renting – mostly in housing association property and unemployed – segregation into a 'special needs' category was a key problem. This could mean segregation into poor areas.

'I think this area is very rough… we've got bars on every single window… attempted burglaries… they had five attempts… with three break-ins… They tended to put people with special needs and we had one or two people that caused problems… and two or three of them have been sectioned since.' (Jo)

Personal safety could become an overriding anxiety after such incidents.

'I used to feel a lot safer when the dog was here… keep myself active… taking the dog out… since I've been broken in, I don't sleep.' (Martin)

Housing benefits and work

How could respondents in social housing find jobs with income and security to meet their costs? Or, if they had jobs, how could they afford the rent of accessible social housing? Housing benefits, which have replaced subsidies to social housing, are a crucial extension of means-testing among disabled people. Housing association properties could be seen as a useful step towards independence, establishing independent living first and moving on to paid employment.

'When I had first moved in here I thought… get yourself established first… Now I have done that I'm bored. I want to do something.' (Amos)

But most of our respondents in social housing felt trapped, facing the loss of their Housing Benefit, by the high rents of accessible housing association properties and the difficulty of finding accessible cheaper housing.

'My main concern is that if employment ends then I will be back to square one… once I start earning some money then it might affect where I have to live because the rent on this place is quite steep.' (Ben)

Becoming self-employed and working from home might protect from a discriminatory labour market. But this route was blocked for Shauna by her housing association rules.

'I would like a box-room so that I can work in there. One of the rules in my tenancy agreement was that I can't set up a business from this location. It drives me up the wall… all I'll be doing like working on my computer and I do that every day so what's the difference.' (Shauna)

The alternative trap was to get the job first, but at the cost of still living with parents. Fran could not access appropriate housing without giving up work.

'We got offered one of these bungalows, and they are lovely. Guess how much rent was? 73 pounds a week… and I would have had to pay that purely because I work… everyone else gets it for nothing.'

Social housing through housing associations provided access, secure tenure and quality service, sometimes combined with valued

personal assistance. For a few it was a route
to fuller independent living. But for most it
was a cul-de-sac, from which it was difficult
to move on either to owner occupation or
to jobs which could support the rents.

Independent householding

Young disabled adults talked about having
their own place, in much the same way as
might their non-disabled peers. Will described
his decision to move out in everyone's interests
when he did not get on well with his mother's
new partner.

> *'It has given me independence to do
> whatever I wanted.'*

Living with parents could seem like a failure
to grow up, and damaging to self-esteem.

> *'I drive, I work full-time, but I still live at
> home, so in some people's eyes, I've not
> made it in the world yet because I still
> live at home. Could be a millionairess as
> well... but I'm still living at home so
> therefore... I'm not worth anything.'* (Fran)

Disabled children are more likely to be
protected, to have less independence,
being at home alone, and more parental
surveillance (Hirst & Baldwin, 1994). Some
respondents still living with parents were
trapped by the difficulty of meeting their
needs out of inadequate income from
employment. But others had not reached the
point of trying for independent living, aware
of the scale of the problems they faced
practically and emotionally.

> *'I don't think I could handle it... able-
> bodied people are becoming independent
> around my age... breaking the ties with
> their parents, but with disabled people,
> those bonds are a lot stronger, and so it*

> *takes a lot more effort... it's very,
> very difficult indeed.'* (Steve)

Social divisions

We have already indicated that young women
from ethnic minorities might meet special
difficulty in parting from parents (**Chapter 2**).
Some respondents met opposition from
parents to any plan to live independently.

> *'My parents wouldn't let me move out...
> they did say to me one day... because
> you're not married you're supposed to be
> living with your parents.'* (Meena)

Conclusion

Becoming a householder is a key aspect of
adulthood and of independent living. We had
respondents with homes of their own, in
neighbourhoods of their choice, with access
and adaptations that met their needs and
enabled their employment, leisure and
participation in society. But they were rare,
the product of exceptional circumstances
or schemes rather than of systems which
favoured them. More of our respondents were
in social housing – usually through housing
associations – which met their access needs
and offered valued services, but usually at the
cost of living on benefits rather than in work.

Few of our respondents had both secure
housing and secure work. There was a
virtuous circle of good enough work to pay
for good enough accommodation, but it was
very difficult to enter. Respondents in jobs
expressed degrees of housing stress in
achieving accessible accommodation
which enabled them to work, move, pay for
personal assistance and have friends. They
were struggling against the policy flow of
meeting their needs with special housing.
For respondents without jobs, housing
associations were providing a good service,

23

but locking them outside the magic circle. These respondents lacked the choice, control and flexibility of owner occupation, were trapped on Housing Benefit, and were thus segregated from work and citizenship.

The housing access and job mobility needs of young disabled people with jobs are not being met and are a serious obstacle to employment. Young adults with disabilities need to be able to use social housing as a resource. They often need and welcome schemes which offer some support with living independently. They also need to be able to move through social housing, if they are to live more independently, move off benefits, move into work and move with jobs. Some housing associations had offered mortgage deposits enabling respondents to move on. Entitlement to such help on a national basis would support young disabled people in getting through to mainstream housing.

Chapter Five
Personal assistance

The claim for personal autonomy through personal assistance controlled by disabled people is an essential feature of the disability movement's demand for independent living. Many of our respondents could not leave their parents' homes until they had established a personal assistance package to live as independent adults. This is a serious challenge for young people and for agencies which mean to meet their needs. Control and autonomy have been seen as crucial for people with impairments if they are to avoid being disabled by care (Morris, 1993, 1997). Working conditions for people doing care work are also on the academic agenda (Ungerson, 1997a, 1997b). Official policy is to move away from services managed by local authorities and towards direct payments of cash for disabled people to manage their own assistance, though it is officially recognised that *'most councils and their staff still have fully to absorb and carry through the independent living philosophy'* (SSI, 2000). How do young adults move from parental care and access, fund and manage the personal assistance that enables independent living? How are they affected by the cost constraints that have developed along with the policy rhetoric, limiting the Independent Living Fund (ILF) and increasing charges for local authority services?

Accessing and managing personal assistance

Leaving home, arranging whatever personal support was needed, managing a job and a household – these were all demanding tasks and not always compatible. Matthew had become established with secure care support through a housing association scheme.

> *'The biggest problem for me was getting accommodation and care, because the two don't tend to go together. To get care it's either in a residential home, or you can find accommodation but there is no care. That is what is so unique about this scheme… there is accommodation in the community and total care and they work.'*

Social services did not figure largely in accounts of responsive and flexible care, but there were some very positive accounts.

> *'I'm happy with all the social services that come in at the moment… Me and me mum phoned up the DSM which is the head of the social services for this area. We… told them what I wanted, when I wanted it and they just provided it.'* (Toby)

Agencies and local authorities had often been steps on the way to assistance managed by individuals, but there were problems of personnel and personal relations.

Most independent respondents described the benefits of managing their own care. Sylvia was interestingly placed, as a social worker, to weigh up the balance between her own arrangements and social services. She emphasised personal relationships, and flexibility for herself and her carers.

> 'They've been excellent and they're more like friends now really... with social services home care they'll do this but they won't do that, and they can't guarantee a time and can't guarantee a carer and... with carers that I've got you can just decide... we've got a rota that runs like clockwork on the whole... probably my experience of social work has helped me to get it all sorted out effectively... if it was done through social services you'd need to continually be having them coming in and reviewing your services and there's criteria... it's the flexibility and give and take that's helped it to work for so long really'.

Rachel spoke of the importance of good relationships with people who share life intimately.

> 'Not only have they sort of got to fit into my lifestyle, they've got to fit in with the family as well, because we are a close family, you know, we do lots of things together, we always eat together, you know, so you have to become part of the family... it's far better to have your own control.'

Steve, who had Community Service Volunteers, found it...

> '...like being married to two people, simultaneously, and you've got to keep... them both happy'.

Respondents spoke of the need for good pay and unexploitative working conditions to underpin good personal assistance.

> 'If you want care which is absolutely suitable for you and is actually the best of the sort of help that you actually want, you have to do it privately and you have to pay the money that that comes with that.' (John)

Managing personal assistance had its own problems: inappropriate employees, unreliable agencies and the strain of managing a payroll, tax, insurance, rotas, fluctuating needs, at the same time as a job. Spontaneity was a big issue.

> 'If disabled people need personal care they have to fit around their carers, so in a lot of ways they haven't got as much freedom as some people would think they have.' (Ann)

Schemes that relieved the burdens of management were welcomed by some respondents, sometimes as a route to managing for themselves.

> 'Because it is part of a scheme we employ a manager who does all the day-to-day stuff so we don't have the hassle of being employers.' (Matthew)

But even our most independent respondents lived with a state of fragile control over day-to-day life. Kate felt that her balance was about to tip away from paid employment as she faced the need for more assistance and acknowledged the work involved in managing it.

> 'I've tried to get away from that, but I'm really really not looking to having all those responsibilities... it might come to a stage where I'm going to have to... especially as my impairment is progressive and going to need more support in the future... I might

say to hell with work, I've got enough work to do that....' (Kate)

Respondents living independently without jobs sometimes felt the demands of care management were work enough.

'Managing personal assistance is a full-time job. If you were employed as well as doing what I am doing you would have no social life.' (Simon)

It may be that our over-representation of people with high care needs among those living independently and unemployed can be understood in terms of the difficulties of managing – and funding – personal assistance while in jobs.

Paying for personal assistance

Financing this kind of care meant a well-paid job or state support, or both. Respondents with these were well aware that they were privileged among disabled peers, especially if they had funding under the original ILF, as did Rachel.

'I'm lucky because I've got ILF funding.'

There were few accounts of employer support, despite our trawl through blue-chip companies and social service departments.

'I have somebody who comes in to work at lunchtimes to help me with my lunch. My employer pays for this and I pay my driver and I contribute towards my care here.' (Matthew)

Benefits, charges and the question of how to cover their care needs loomed large for respondents who were living independently but not working. Phil 'talked about going for work' but feared losing essential benefits.

'We wouldn't get us care provided, we'd have to fund that ourselves, and we wouldn't get any help with it... I'd say that's a restriction.'

Mark talked of home help charges and the...

'...need for the right amount of money coming in... to enable you to, to exist, or to have a good quality of life... part of me (Mark) *will say yes, tomorrow, I'd love to get a job... working with computers, but financially there's not that money out there.'*
(See **Chapter 7**.)

Parents and personal care

Respondents living with parents were likely to have their personal assistance needs met by their parents. For some this meant responsive, flexible and familiar support.

'If they're coming in at certain times... I'd find it hard to live like that... I like to be spontaneous, I like to be flexible... I think it's an advantage because it's my mum doing it.' (Helen)

Where mothers were doing skilled nursing work, this was especially difficult to replace.

'Because of my spina bifida and where it is, my mum cleans my back out for me... when in the past my mum's not been able to do it, and people have come in, it's not been done properly.' (Ruth)

'In fact she's taking care of me really, I can't do anything... she does everything for me, it's brilliant. There's no-one better to look after you than your mum really... because nurses, while they know what's wrong, they don't know everything.' (Alice)

Isabel thought it …

> '…would be quite scary to move out, cos you're close to your mum, so you don't really feel intimidated or embarrassed when your mum helps you'.

Michelle echoes her anxiety about exchanging the security of the care they knew for strangers.

> 'Getting to know them… to start off they are going to be strangers aren't they, doing weird things for me… I've got to do it.'

But parental care could be damaging to parents.

> 'Now I'm getting older… they shouldn't be doing it… they are both in their fifties… Lifting me is not safe for them and that's what concerns me really.' (Michelle)

It could also be a problem for respondents, postponing adulthood.

> 'My dad does quite a lot of intimate personal care, and I don't like that… I don't think he can quite see it from my point of view because I don't think he accepts that I'm an adult. They don't want to let me go. And they don't want to admit that they've looked after me inappropriately… my dad being my carer'. (Tracey)

All our respondents with learning disabilities were living at home with their parents who met their personal assistance needs.

Conclusion

Choice about personal assistance is an essential component of adulthood. We had respondents who had this kind of choice – though it was often hard-won and fragile. But we also had respondents living at home with parents who had never had the simplest control over day-to-day life. Those respondents who were daunted by the problems of replacing their mothers' skilled nursing support have little choice now and risk nursing-home care in the future.

The policy rhetoric of autonomy and control for people with impairments conformed broadly with many of our respondents' aspirations for independent living. Most of our most independent respondents spoke more enthusiastically of managing their own assistance than of any alternative. It gave control over relationships in terms of whom they let into their lives and how far, flexibility to meet changing needs as they saw fit and autonomy in day-to-day life. But it took time to achieve and was not a panacea. Few could move straight from living at home with parental care to taking effective control over personal assistance. Schemes in which others did the managing – including traditional social service provision for some – reduced the labour and could be made to fit the complex demands of these lives. Schemes which included the crucial package of housing and personal assistance were described warmly by some respondents. Employers were making little contribution. Information and support in accessing, funding and managing personal assistance beyond the family need to be much more general.

In the face of means tests and charges, it has become difficult for people with assistance needs to combine autonomy in personal care with employment. The problems of funding personal assistance were a serious barrier to adulthood: a barrier to work, a barrier to independent householding and a barrier to growing away from dependent relationships with parents. The personal assistance trap set by charges needs addressing urgently for young people growing up with impairment, if their support needs are not to be an impassable barrier to adulthood.

Chapter Six
Work

'Work for those who can' (DSS, 1998) is the current official slogan. Many respondents were clear about their abilities and desire to work. We asked about supports to employment, but it was difficult to avoid answers which exploded with difficulties: a hostile labour market, discriminatory employers, limited support for personal assistance and access needs, and how to earn enough to cover costs.

Radical post-war legislation in the *Disabled Person's (Employment) Act* of 1944 addressed the labour market, imposing a quota of a 3% disabled workforce on employers. This attempt to influence the social organisation of work chimes with the disability movement's much later emphasis on disabling structures, but it was disregarded by employers and prosecutors. The policy trend has been away from the labour market, officially abandoning the quota in 1996, and towards individuals. Now the *Disability Discrimination Act* of 1995 gives individual rights through individual processes and the New Deal for Disabled People in 1998 adds to them (Barnes, 2000; Roulstone, 1998; Hyde, 2000). There is a powerful argument that the labour market has been marginalising disabled people further in the past two decades. If so, the New Deal may aid individuals but is unlikely to transform employment prospects for the many. Return-to-work policies are being aimed at nearly two million disabled people and two million others (Berthoud, 1998 p40).

Workforce-centred remedies – old and new – assist a few thousand people annually. The New Deal so far has (in 15 months) accepted 3,000 disabled people on to innovative programmes and placed just over 2,000 in jobs, tending to help those with least need (Millar, 2000).

Adult status and paid employment

For many respondents with jobs, employment was central to their sense of themselves as adults. Robert talked of work as life itself.

> 'I got to thinking clearly. And I thought you've got a choice, start work and just do it. Or you can just get in the corner and just die, can't you?'

Toby described work as daily activity and independence.

> 'I like to have independence and do my own thing. I don't like to sit in the flat all day and do nothing. I like to… be active.'

Jo talked of career and friends.

> 'I've built up quite a good career in the media; most of my friends have good jobs here…'

…and John of self-esteem – *'I feel much, much more self-confident'* – and control.

For Diane work gave…

> '…*financial independence from my*
> (Diane's) *family and my fiancé and*
> *I think that is the most valuable thing'* .

It also gave money to *'buy what I want…*
go where I want to… I wouldn't want to give
that up'.

For Mike a job brought equality in society.

> *'Being an adult and not being treated as*
> *different because you have a disability*
> *but being treated as an equal person.'*

Employment did not have to be paid to bring
some of the same rewards; some respondents
talked of voluntary work in similar terms.
But the low incomes of those without jobs
brought exclusion from the daily lives of
their peers.

> *'My friends they got cars, they got houses,*
> *they got jobs and… I'm the odd one out…*
> *I'm different enough without that as*
> *well… I can't compete with their style of*
> *living… they can go out and spend about*
> *fifty pounds a night, they can go out to*
> *the pub.'* (Martin)

And for Martin, exclusion from the labour
market was the most wounding of many
barriers to being like other people.

> *'I think society makes you feel more,*
> *sort of alienated, if you like, cos you can't,*
> *you want to be more like everybody else…*
> *I used to have a dream that I learned to*
> *drive, had my own house, but until I can*
> *get a job, then… that's a bit impossible.'*

So for respondents with jobs, employment
gave them daily activity, self-confidence,
independence, control over day-to-day life,
a place in society, consumption, an escape
from the stigma of claiming benefits and
concomitant sense of identity as an equal
citizen. If these were stereotypical accounts
of work in young adults' lives in general, they
were also suffused with the sense of an
alternative disabled destiny without them.
Paid employment was widely seen by
respondents in jobs and out as the key to
adult status and participation in society on
an equal basis with non-impaired peers.

Supporting transition to work

Transition to work posed problems which
some resolved as individuals by offering
themselves for a trial period for no pay or
for below market rates.

> *'It's just not geared for the actual transition*
> *into work. A lot of work needs to be done*
> *on considering practical needs. People who*
> *are disabled may need a trial period of*
> *work to potentially open out future*
> *employment possibilities… I was working*
> *for next to nothing… out in the big wide*
> *world I could have expected to earn thirty*
> *grand a year. The company wanted to see*
> *what I could do. In the end they saw what*
> *I could do and they loved it.'* (John)

Sandwich placements on university courses
were another solution. Matthew, who was one
of the highest earners in the sample (and
among the most severely impaired),
described this strategy.

> *'The year's placement was in a council,*
> *and because they knew me and knew my*
> *work they were able to create a place for*
> *me. I have been there eight years.'*

Government schemes played a small role
for our respondents. The New Deal was not
mentioned, though three had used a Youth

Training Scheme or supported employment scheme. These led to low-paid jobs.

> *'I went on a YTS scheme when I left school, working in an accounts department. I knew my figure work was good and that I could do certain tasks that were set for me. I was on the scheme for two years.'* (Paul)

Voluntary sector employment schemes were valued for supporting transition to work, providing skills, and leading to better paid employment. Graduate training programmes administered by the larger disability organisations in conjunction with a number of major employers assisted three respondents.

> *'I think it was very positive for me. It has given me a lot more confidence and it also gave me stability as well, to sort of think about things that I might like to do…*
> *it has been very good.'* (Susan)

Informal networking was the key to employment for several of the better paid respondents, but may be difficult for young disabled people whose social networks may shrink as they grow to adulthood.

Employing disabled people

Our search for well paid and well placed disabled workers produced some results. Our sample contained people with responsible jobs in information technology working as computer programmers, IT advisers and systems analysts, and respondents in careers, media or social service occupations. Nine respondents earned above the national average of £21, 842. But, as any reading of the literature would lead us to expect, the majority were in poorly paid jobs such as basic data entry and riveting the handles on mushroom baskets. Among our 31 most

independent respondents, 18 were earning less than £15,000, as well as 10 of the 12 working and living at home.

The public sector was crucial as an employer, especially for higher earners. Professional qualifications in teaching and social work gave respondents access to career paths and to employers who were more likely to be disability-aware, enabling essential equipment, access and occasionally personal assistance. Self-employment offered three respondents an alternative route to freedom from disabling environments, but into low-paid work.

Enabling employers were described across all sectors.

> *'Your average teacher will probably raise their eyebrows a little bit at the idea of someone blind trying to teach kids, but where I work they think that I can do everything… The headmaster has been brilliant and he has given me… just perfect support really.'* (Ian)

Danielle liked her pushy, private sector employment where…

> *'…the people are brilliant, they are very up with training and being up-to-date with everything'*.

But there was little in the accounts to suggest that private sector employers in general are enabling employment among people with impairments.

Access at work

Physical access needs were, occasionally, met readily.

> *'I had very much the support that I needed. The building had a ramp at the front and there was an accessible toilet. I had a hoist*

put in the loo within two months of being there and various electric doors are now in the building. I've been very lucky.' (Jo)

But even respondents in good jobs described repeated humiliating and debilitating access problems.

'When I first moved to the job we were based in a building on the second floor, there were no lifts so I was isolated downstairs in a room by myself. It took two years to get all the adaptations done, and when I suggested that I was thinking of moving the response was "but we have just had the disabled toilet done".' (Sylvia)

'I work on the first floor and there are only two disabled toilets, on the ground floor and in the basement, and I have to drink a lot of water. I used to have to write down every time I went to the toilet and how long it took.' (Danielle)

The funding and quality of personal assistance and the difficulties with charges (**Chapter 5**) were key issues for respondents at work.

Equipment for work

Equipment needs, usually for technology or accessible information formats, could be provided through disability service teams (previously PACTs). Jo was among a small group who found that *'the employment services have been excellent'*. Technology was crucial to Richard's job.

'I do a lot of work on the computer. I have a large VDU and a couple of magnifiers.'

For most employed respondents, these crucial needs were met with great difficulty, delays and detriment to their work and relations with colleagues.

'I have been trying to sort some speech equipment out, but so far it has been a right mess. It has been going on for three years so far. Getting quotes for equipment and finding out if the council or PACT are funding it have proved very difficult. Without this equipment people who I need to talk to need a personal computer handy instead of me having something on my wheelchair and just talking where we are.' (Tom)

'When I was working in admin I was left sitting around for a minimum of six weeks waiting for equipment to arrive, feeling very much like a spare part, not being able to get on with my job. Everybody was saying "what is that person supposed to be doing?".' (Sally)

Nobody employed in the private sector had received any such assistance. Delays in essential equipment left Chloe doing routine work.

'The equipment that I need has still not arrived so I am spending my time doing the photocopying. I feel so isolated.'

Tim argued that public support was biased against large private companies…

'…because they are seen as having a large amount of money and that is a very negative attitude as far as I'm concerned. That is them trying to use a "get out of jail card" which is not right, given the amount of money that they have to spend. OK, I work for a big organisation, but money is as tight as anywhere else and there is even more pressure for me to provide a business case. I have to justify my existence as soon as anybody else. PACT works on the principle that I have been employed as a purely philanthropic gesture'.

Such difficulties were more often found among private sector employees, but disability organisations in the voluntary sector were not immune to criticism.

> 'We are meant to be teaching the world and we don't practise what we preach.'

Training and promotion

Training and promotion were more often raised as difficulties than as opportunities.

> 'I was left in the job to learn the job. My experience in the first 14 months was abysmal, it was disorganised. It is only now three years later, that I feel I am receiving the recognition that I should have been… Only by my own intervention have I got to the stage that the job I'm in I'm relatively happy with. There is a major gap in what the company perceives it provides and what it actually provides.'
> (Alison)

Deterrents to employment

Most of our respondents in the comparative groups felt capable of work. A few had left jobs after ill health or poor workplace support. More had tried and failed to find employment. Most would prefer paid employment. There were three key deterrents to employment: lack of educational qualifications, failed applications and – looming largest – financial problems, especially in relation to benefits for personal assistance.

Siresh focused on qualifications.

> 'There is not much hope for employment because you have got to have a good education and I haven't.'

More emphasised employer attitudes.

> 'You could be highly qualified and have something like a degree, and be more qualified than the other person who is going for the same job, but at the end of the day the employer is most likely to take the able-bodied person over you because it is going to cause the employer problems to take a disabled person.' (Sam)

The prospect of losing essential benefits – especially personal assistance benefits – was critical for every respondent who had not actively sought employment. Income Support, Housing Benefit and Council Tax were also concerns, but it was easier to imagine earning enough to cover these than personal care.

> 'As far as Income Support or any of those benefits goes I'm happy to give up those benefits for some kind of employment… but if a person is entitled to personal care benefits then they should be entitled to it regardless of whether they work or don't work.' (Siresh)

Parental support

Living at home with parents was one solution to the personal assistance trap, especially for people on low pay, though only for people not needing assistance at work. With parents to provide any care needed at home and cover some household costs, respondents could survive on very low incomes. Five respondents living at home were earning below £10,000. Frank acknowledged:

> '…if I had to have personal assistance I could not afford to work. I have got a fairly good job, although the money is not brilliant, but I just wish that they would give disabled people the same opportunities as everybody else'.

Such a solution brought adult status as a worker. But it was likely to postpone the achievement of independent housing and independent living, with low earnings unlikely to cover rent and personal assistance.

Social divisions

Our women respondents were under-represented in the independent living/employed group and over-represented in those employed but living with parents. While no statistical significance can be drawn from our samples, our greater difficulty in finding women respondents employed and living independently may well reflect women's lower earnings and greater difficulty with meeting costs – especially the costs of personal assistance.

Conclusion

> *'The best thing that I ever did was go out to work, because along with a career there comes a social life as well, you know, and I would dread to think of sitting at home or going to a day centre. That would kill me off. I just couldn't do it.'* (Rachel)

> *'It's wanting to work and being able to work – two different things there.'* (Martin)

These respondents – Rachel in employment and Martin on benefit – illustrate similar attitudes to employment. There was widespread feeling among our respondents that paid work was the best route away from poverty and social exclusion and into other aspects of adulthood – social relationships and citizenship – but even those in the better jobs tended to describe the work environment as hostile. There were supports for transition to employment and they need to be much more widespread. Personal assistance might be enabled by employers, but it was very rare, and we found none in the private sector.

To work equally with their peers, these young adults need public non-means-tested support for their personal assistance. Essential equipment was sometimes provided by the employment service, but respondents reported obstructive difficulties between public providers and private employers. Again, young disabled adults need public support if they are to work equally with their peers. But – as increasingly with support for personal assistance – it needs to become a direct payment to disabled people, a government-funded entitlement paid through an independent body such as the ILF. An endowment for transition to work would put young adults in control of meeting their own equipment needs, at a stage when they often have no personal or family resources. Our respondents did not feel that employers in competitive environments should be expected to provide for access and assistance needs, but they do need employers to provide work.

Chapter Seven
Benefits

Benefits are a very significant element in disabled people's incomes, even for many in employment. Higher living costs, personal assistance needs and greater vulnerability to low pay and unemployment may all give rise to benefit entitlements, which are likely to form over half household income (Burchardt, 2000b p51). Increasing recognition of extra costs through the non-means-tested Disability Living Allowance has been one favourable policy trend for people with disabilities – especially if they want and can find work (Berthoud, 1998 p67). A second policy trend is to increase disabled people's control of their personal assistance through the 1996 *Community Care (Direct Payments) Act* (which costs less to local authorities) (Dawson, 2000 p46). A third policy trend, of increasing charges for personal assistance, is creating a personal assistance trap to add to the poverty and unemployment traps (Kestenbaum, 1997, 1998, 1999).

Welfare-to-work policies may improve prospects of employment and the rewards from it for some, while posing risks to others of being cast as undeserving (Burchardt, 2000b p42). The majority not working may be entitled to means-tested Income Support. It is now policy to recognise – modestly – the needs of people who have grown up with impairment, through targeting Severe Disablement Allowance on them. Most respondents engage with the benefit system and are subject to benefit policy and practice. Whether benefits are means tested or not, how benefits are withdrawn as earnings rise, how benefits are withdrawn as earnings rise,

whether services attract charges, how different benefit and charging regimes around income support, housing and personal assistance add up – these are key issues. The broad picture from the policy literature is of disabled people's vulnerability to poverty and social exclusion (Morris, 2001) and of a benefit system that is disabling rather than enabling. Some of the policy trends may offer an improving environment for disabled people reaching adulthood. What is their experience of the benefit system?

Meeting higher costs through the Disability Living Allowance

The higher costs of disabled living for all respondents were met in part through Disability Living Allowance. This has a 'mobility component' and a 'care' component (at different levels, according to degree of impairment) and is the key non-means-tested benefit available to disabled people with jobs. For respondents in employment, especially if they had independent households too, it was a crucial bedrock.

> *'DLA makes a hell of a difference... the fact that it's not means-tested and it's always there to use as a form of security.'* (Kathy)

For Tim, who was *'paid a manager's wage, doing a manager's job'*, it offered mobility and a sense of fairness.

*'I can't afford to run a car on my wages…
I do feel that I need the mobility
component because it does provide
somewhat of a level playing field…
unless you're paid megabucks there's
no way you can get away from the
fundamental principle that there has
to be some low level of support to
enable that disability.'* (Tim)

Lucy was able to combine DLA with reduced hours.

*'I didn't feel I could physically do
a 9–5 job… so I'm doing 10–3…
but I still get my benefit on top so
it's all worked out great.'* (Lucy)

But it is a modest benefit, and respondents did not find it adequate to cover the costs resulting from mobility impairment or personal assistance needs.

*'There should be a minimum…
to cover the extra needs. Disability
Living Allowance should be double
what it is now to cope with those
extra costs.'* (Eddie)

Paul's pay, with DLA, just covered his rent and assistance in a housing association scheme and left him about £40 to live on. Everyone else in the scheme was on means-tested benefits and paid a lot less. But this was still liberty.

*'I have my freedom now, to do what
I want, when I want, where I want,
with whom I want and how.'* (Paul)

Benefits for personal assistance

Personal assistance needs were a significant issue for people in employment. A few respondents paid for assistance out of

earnings – Catherine received DLA but working has *'enabled me* (Catherine) *to carry on paying for my carers and that sort of thing'* – but most needed support to fund personal assistance.

DLA's 'care component' is small in relation to the costs of full-time personal assistance and, it is usually agreed, is not intended to cover this kind of support. Several respondents looked to the Independent Living Fund and/or local authorities to meet their personal assistance needs, but had their DLA care component means-tested. As earlier chapters have shown, this creates a personal assistance trap which is a major hindrance to work for young adults with severe impairments. This trap consists of *'two main elements. One is the sheer complexity of the systems of benefits, community care and employment support which a person has to negotiate if they need personal assistance at home and work. The second is means-testing for social care, which leads to situations where people in employment, often in full-time, skilled and demanding jobs, are as little as £30 a week better off than if unemployed and claiming Income Support'* (Kestenbaum, 1998 p69).

Respondents with personal assistance needs felt more vulnerable to bureaucratic decision-making than did those who could manage without. Tom's life was underpinned by the ILF, but he had great anxieties about meeting new legal requirements for his assistants – holiday pay for part-time workers – while depending on ILF decisions.

*'I asked the ILF for a wage increase and
they basically deducted my money.'*

It is, then, particularly difficult for young adults with personal assistance needs to negotiate the means-test environment of the Independent Living Funds and local authority direct payments schemes and to enter employment.

Into work

Transition to work was highlighted as a problem, especially the transition to work paying less than benefits and which might be insecure. Three respondents were claiming Disability Working Allowance as an earnings supplement, but no-one discussed it except to criticise its restrictions. Its new life as the Disabled Person's Tax Credit (from October 1999) brings more generous conditions and support, which may make it more useful to disabled people seeking work.

Robert had part-funding from social services which supported his employment.

> '*Social services pay 35% of my salary... companies could get this part-funding to... get firms just to start me. Just to say that I'm not stupid or to get a start somewhere. And that has worked.*'

Some respondents who had made careers were able to take the longer view. Rachel made her own transition scheme. She had found it a worry to lose benefits when she started work, and gave her employers a trial period of three weeks unpaid...

> '*...to see whether I could do the job and for them to see whether I could do the job... for the first couple or three years it was probably costing me more to go to work than it would have done staying at home... I've got promotion and over the years it's got better*'. (Rachel)

Transition from a first job to work that would pay more than benefits could be prolonged, involving long periods of living with high costs and low incomes, but giving independence, higher incomes and a richer life in the longer term.

> '*Now my first job was part-time and it wasn't very good money and I did lose my benefit... now I'm a lot better off than I've ever been in my life.*' (Eddie)

> '*Having done both... it's much better to work, it really is, there are things I've done in this job that I wouldn't have been able to do on Income Support.*' (David)

These respondents focused on the rewards of paid employment, financial and otherwise, but also highlighted risks they had come through. Saul thought other disabled people should take the long view.

> '*I was worse off coming off benefits... I think it's a mistake people often make when they say I am £20 worse off a week by taking a job... are they ever going to be well off living on benefits?*'

But he admitted basing his own decision on a miscalculation, and the risks of transition to work will be higher for some disabled people than for others – higher for those without parental resources, those with personal assistance needs, those facing further discrimination in the labour market through ethnicity or gender and those whose educational qualifications give them poor career prospects.

Living on means-tested benefits

Benefits played a much larger part in the lives and comments of those without employment. They were likely to be receiving Income Support or other income replacement benefits as well as DLA, sometimes Independent Living Fund and local authority support for personal assistance needs and adaptations and housing benefits. Respondents were very aware of the costs and risks attached to employment and of the limitations of their own earning capacity.

No-one loved living on means-tested benefits, but it did give them a secure income which bore some relation to their extra needs, whereas they were well aware that working would bring them an insecure income which could well be inversely related to their needs as disabled people.

Poor rewards from work were stressed by those who felt poorly qualified, like Samantha.

'…lack of qualifications… the sort of job that I'm able to do wouldn't coincide with losing my benefits…'

and Tania.

'Because I didn't have any qualifications when I left school, there was no real hope of employment… I don't particularly want to be on benefit. But it would have to be something that… would pay a decent wage.'

The insecurity of work combined with the certainty of higher costs, especially with personal assistance.

'I need to make sure that I'm covered because of my costs. I mean I'm used to money I can rely on… I personally don't think it's right that if you get a job you lose your independent living allowance [ILF]*… because you are still having to live independently and it's a lot tougher than anybody else.'* (Michelle)

Respondents who were living independently and derived their main income from benefits recounted costs for personal assistance, housing, mobility or adaptations. Mobility costs were central for Mark.

'I would like to work but it would have to be a really decent amount of money…

the motorbike… things like that are very expensive because they're built to order… six and a half grand, not a lot of people can afford that amount of money… the main thing stopping people from working is the financial aspect of it.'

Adaptations, which she counted at £10,000, were a big issue for Simone. Housing costs and the prospect of losing Housing Benefit added to the problem for respondents renting from housing associations.

The increasing value of DLA was an important bridge to employment for some respondents, but not enough in general to enable young adults to take jobs. Respondents living mainly on means-tested benefits enjoyed the increasing autonomy brought by independent living, but were constrained by the (essentially contradictory) policies of means-tests and charges on local authority services. They may have been more averse to risk than their employed counterparts – and perhaps more exposed to risk through lower earning capacity – but their attitudes to work did not seem divergent.

'I do a lot of voluntary work instead, so I feel that I am putting back into the community in my own way. But ideally I would like a proper wage so that I can say that I am earning – it is a sense of achievement.' (Martin)

Citizenship

Many respondents had a highly developed sense of themselves as citizens. Some respondents described themselves as active citizens, working for the disability movement, doing voluntary work. Others discussed their notions of state welfare. The disability movement has tended to make young people more aware of disability as a social, political and economic phenomenon (Tisdall, 2000).

Experience of the benefit system looms large in many respondents' accounts of their lives. Most have been obliged to think about their relationship with state welfare systems and notions of stigma, rights, free-riding, incentives to work and responsibility to society.

Disability has exposed respondents to the risk of being stigmatised as dependent. Experience with the benefit system has often been degrading. Some respondents expressed a strong desire to be seen as contributing to society rather than free-riding on it.

> '*I wanted to be earning a living, to be independent… not relying on other people to provide financial support for you, but standing on your own two feet.*' (Mike)

> '*It makes me feel good that I don't have to call on somebody else to pay to keep me here, to keep me in food and clothes.*' (John)

There were well-developed views about the incentives offered by the benefit system, the kinds of benefit that were needed to support them as independent adults and the reality – or otherwise – of the benefit system as a disincentive to adequately paid work if they could get it.

> '*If somebody's just going out, and earning a basic wage, you're not gonna be able to live on that and to provide care for yourself… So… that's not right, because that will just put the person off going to work, if it's too much of a struggle for them… they can't afford to live, they can't afford to get the care, then the easy option for most people is to live off the Government. Whereas it's all right if you've got a job that pays you enough money to do that.*' (Helen)

There was a widespread sense that, as young disabled adults, they could support themselves better with more support from welfare systems and especially benefit systems. It did not seem fair to have to pay for personal assistance just because they had an impairment and a job, and it did seem fair that they should be supported with transport when impairment limited their mobility.

> '*The things you claim from the Government help towards what you need, for example a car, which is my independence basically. Because… my legs wouldn't walk me everywhere.*' (Helen)

Most did not think that a generous benefit system would deter people from work, if work could only be found – though there were critical accounts of peers: '*friends… who are perfectly capable of working but just won't*' (Fran).

There was widespread frustration about the failure of the benefit system to support independence.

> '*Claiming benefit… is not necessarily directed towards sensible use of resources, independent living, going on to work… it's geared if anything completely against that at all levels.*' (Kathy)

Dan articulated a position about welfare benefits that was widely held by respondents. Respondents felt that compensation for their impairments would be fair and justified, but they also wanted to be treated with equal respect.

> '*I want my rights as a disabled person. I want to be normal but I want my rights.*' (Dan)

Conclusion

Our respondents, even those with qualifications, had long periods of low incomes and high risk to establish themselves in rewarding careers. The increasing value of benefits to compensate for extra costs – represented by DLA – was a significant support to them and to their decision to work. Welfare-to-work policies may help further in future. But increasing means-testing has impacted especially hard upon these respondents. Income Support, Housing Benefit and means-tested housing adaptations, personal assistance charges – these make a cumulative means-testing environment which inhibits transition to adulthood, preventing movement from parental care to personal autonomy, through specialised housing/housing benefit into owner occupation and from unemployment into work.

In this means-testing environment, achieving one transition could inhibit the others. Becoming independent of parental care may mean adopting personal assistance, with charges that inhibit work. Becoming a householder may mean accepting housing association property, with rents which cannot be covered through earnings. Taking a job while living at home may hinder finding accessible affordable housing or personal assistance that is independent of parents.

Benefit structures made it difficult to stage transitions to adulthood. These difficulties were compounded when respondents also lacked confidence in themselves as adults. The tiny minority who took jobs and made independent lives were exceptional in their choice and opportunity and did so in defiance of the benefit system.

Disability Living Allowance was the key benefit which consistently supported transition to adulthood, including transition to work. It needs to be strengthened. It should be protected against local authority charges for personal assistance, to enable paid employment on a more equal basis for people with impairments. It could also have more generous eligibility criteria for the higher rates. It could be enhanced with a premium for those growing up with impairment, who often come through poverty in childhood and arrive at adult years with few resources. There is now extra support for young people impaired from birth or childhood through the Severe Disablement Allowance, but it is aimed at those not in paid work. Young people growing up with impairment and wanting to work have to sacrifice SDA; there is nothing in the benefits system to acknowledge their extra needs and support their decision to work. Stronger support through DLA would help these young adults into work and help them to support themselves.

Chapter Eight
Conclusion

Achieving an independent adulthood integrated with the life of their non-disabled peers in jobs, independent households, social life and citizenship is very difficult for young people who have grown up with impairments. The idea behind our research was to find respondents who had grown up with impairments, but yet had achieved key aspects of adulthood, and to explore what lay behind their achievements. This aim was undermined at all stages. First we struggled to find a sample – and travelled far to do so. Our approach to major employers, public and private, brought plenty of polite interest, but few with employees with significant impairments from birth or childhood. Second, it was difficult to engage respondents with the supports rather than the difficulties. While they often shared their triumphs, they had little to say about any supportive structures. There were much more consistent – and impassioned – accounts of obstacles to adulthood. Third, these were exceptional people giving accounts of exceptional circumstances – of extraordinary parents, of resources from a medical negligence case, of a mother's death triggering appropriate support outside the family. They gave no account of a general network of supports for respondents growing to adulthood. Where housing authorities, social services departments or voluntary agencies had offered crucial support, we often have only two or three respondents to describe them. It is, then, easier to write about the difficulties than it is about the supports to transition to adulthood for young disabled people.

Combining different aspects of adult status is especially difficult. Few young people who have grown up with an impairment have employment as well as independent households, especially if they need personal assistance. A few respondents had jobs that paid enough to give them choices about housing, personal assistance, social relationships and activities, a sense of being part of society in general rather than a society of disability, and a sense of contributing as full citizens. Most respondents felt able to work, saw employment as the key to other aspects of adulthood and would have been pleased with jobs that enabled them to support themselves. Many respondents accepted independent living without employment, not as a choice, but as an achievable independence which was supported by benefit and housing systems and which buffered them from some risks.

Respondents described stereotypical aspirations for growing up, achieving independence through employment, householding and social relationships, with independent transport and control over daily life figuring larger than it might among non-disabled peers.

'I hoped that I would have a job that I liked doing and get married and have kids. And that's sort of where I am at the minute.' (David)

Some respondents had full lives as adults, including marriage and children, but, despite our best efforts to find them, they were rare. Robert reminds us that adulthood for most young people also involves social life.

> 'I've got my house. I've got my car.
> I've got my job. I go to the pub for
> a drink – there's a lot of people in
> the pub that I know. I get to parties.'

Aspirations among our least independent respondents were often much more limited. Jenny would be pleased with a small measure of control over daily life.

> 'Independence – does not necessarily mean
> leaving home... it would mean that
> I could live my days... without having
> to ask my parents to help me... whether
> that be getting around or using the
> phone... things like that.' (Jenny)

Our respondents with jobs and independent households most often named parents as the key to their achievements. Few found their transition to adulthood supported by structures outside the family. Those with supportive parents were often underpinned through a prolonged period of growing towards independence. But not all have supportive parents and not all parents have such resources – indeed, having a disabled child may have propelled them into poverty. Policy for parental responsibility has tended to remove alternative sources of support. If young disabled people are to grow into independence from families, they need a much more secure network of social supports.

Educational qualifications are an obvious source of labour market advantage for respondents in jobs. But respondents were polarised between the educated minority and the rest. Their experience of segregated education was especially polarised. The movement towards integration is likely to continue, but policy needs to take account of the losses of specialised support and focused resources. It also needs to give much more power to the parents of disabled children to enable them to compete in the mainstream market.

Social housing could be a route to owner occupation via joint ownership or mortgage deposit schemes, but for most the rents made a cul-de-sac, a major part of the difficulty of finding employment that could cover costs. Respondents seeking independence through jobs experienced extreme housing stress. Job mobility, inaccessibility of the general housing stock, the difficulty of finding temporary, transitional accommodation to leave parental homes, or to move to new jobs – all these made the housing lives of our respondents in jobs very difficult. These respondents were working against the policy flow of meeting their needs through social housing. Housing associations, the main source of accessible accommodation for young people leaving their parents' homes, often provided a valued standard of service, sometimes with personal support arrangements. But respondents were not always happy to be part of a 'special needs' community – indeed they often felt unsafe – and rents covered by Housing Benefit were a serious obstacle to work. Schemes supporting young disabled adults to move through social housing could be copied. People growing up with impairments have often reached adulthood without any significant resources. A national mortgage deposit scheme aimed at this group would make a significant contribution to enabling those who want to work to come off Housing Benefit.

Paid work was widely seen as the best route into other aspects of adulthood and away from social exclusion, but even those in the better-paid jobs often described the work environment as hostile. Supports for transition into employment were very erratic. Respondents experienced scepticism from employers about their abilities and the difficulties of employing them. Schemes for supporting transition into work through part-payment of salaries for a period enabled respondents to win employers' confidence. There was no expectation from respondents that private sector employers in a competitive environment could cover the costs of special equipment or personal assistance, and without public support for them, many of our respondents could not expect to be employed. Our respondents needed much freer access to employment supports, especially to work in the private sector. An endowment for transition to work – a state-funded capital sum to spend on equipment – would put them much more in control of meeting their own needs and make a life at work, rather than on benefits, a possibility for more respondents.

Disability Living Allowance, as the key non-means-tested benefit to compensate for higher costs, consistently underpinned employment with independent living. It could be more generous to those impaired from birth or childhood. DLA is especially important to respondents who have grown up with impairment, because they have had little opportunity to build up resources for themselves. It is also especially important for respondents seeking employment, because it is secure income offering some cover for the risks they face in coming off other benefits. The means-testing regime of Income Support, Housing Benefit and charges for personal assistance is a serious obstacle to work for young people with impairments. Respondents might try to use these benefits to become established independently, but they found it very difficult to move on from housing supported by Housing Benefit, personal assistance supported by ILF/local authorities, to their own housing with their

own pay. Benefits supported a life that was reasonably secure, but limiting to bigger aspirations. Recent changes to Severe Disablement Allowance create a precedent for offering more generous support to those impaired in childhood and benefit those not in work. A premium to DLA for those impaired in childhood would benefit mainly those in work. More generous criteria for receipt of DLA, and protecting it against local authority charges, would contribute to a more enabling environment for employment.

Personal assistance can support employment, but in general the need for personal assistance is a major impediment to paid work. Respondents usually preferred to manage their own personal assistance, for the control it gave them over their personal lives and personal space. The ILF and direct payments from social services could support independent living and were critical for autonomous adulthood, enabling some respondents to move on from parental care and live outside institutions. But the growing regime of charges seemed unfair to them and was a serious obstacle to work. Local authorities' charges against their DLA – intended to cover other higher disability living costs – could leave respondents with very low incomes. There needs to be a more equal basis for people with impairments, so that people with personal assistance needs can work and earn like their peers.

Transition is a period of risk for young people in general. These respondents, many with high costs and low resources, were especially exposed to risk. Benefit structures made it difficult to stage them. The most reliable services that reduced risks – Income Support and housing associations – were also services that limited a full adult life. Keeping people for a lifetime on means-tested benefits is a very expensive option for governments and would not be most of our respondents' choice. Choosing work is currently a very tough and expensive option for young people with disabilities, but rewarding for those who achieve it.

Key social divisions among our respondents implied different life chances. Our most independent respondents were much more likely to have parents in higher occupational categories, with social, cultural and economic resources to underpin a prolonged transition to adulthood. There were more men – with men's incomes – combining paid work and independent living than women. Ethnic minorities were well represented in the 'most independent' group, but some women from ethnic minorities described special difficulties with becoming independent: leaving parents who might depend on them and who might resist plans for independent living.

Growing up with impairment is a serious obstacle course. Loosening strong family ties, getting jobs, managing households and personal assistance, developing social lives and intimate relationships and parenthood, attaining a sense of oneself as an equal citizen – all these are more difficult for young people with impairments. People who grow up with impairments may develop no resources for dealing with the world, while developing a sense of a disabled destiny for themselves. There is some recognition dawning in policy circles about the difficulties of growing up with impairment, but neither government nor disability movement has fully acknowledged the obstacles to independence for young people who may reach adult years with few resources. Young disabled people may – if they are very lucky – inherit material capital and cultural capital from parents. But they may not. Few young people with severe impairments will grow into independence without restraints on markets that will otherwise discriminate against them and without social resources beyond the family.

References

Armstrong, F. & Barton, L. (1999) *Disability, Human Rights and Education: Cross-Cultural Perspectives.* London: Jessica Kingsley.

Baldwin, S. (1985) *The Costs of Caring: Families with Disabled Children.* London: Routledge and Kegan Paul.

Baldwin, S. & Carlisle, J. (1994) *Social Support for Disabled Children and their Families: A Review of the Literature.* Edinburgh: HMSO.

Barnes, C. (2000) A working social model? Disability, work and disability politics in the 21st century. *Disability and Society* **20** (4) 441–458.

Beresford, B. (1994) *Positively Parents: Caring for a Severely Disabled Child.* London: HMSO.

Beresford, B. (2000) *Expert Opinions: A National Survey of Parents Caring for a Severely Disabled Child.* Bristol: The Policy Press, in association with the Joseph Rowntree Foundation and *Community Care.*

Beresford, B. & Oldman, C. (2000) *Making Homes Fit for Children: Working Together to Promote Change in the Lives of Disabled Children.* Bristol: The Policy Press.

Berthoud, R. (1998) *Disability Benefit.* York: York Publishing Services/Joseph Rowntree Foundation.

Bull, R. (2000) *Housing Options for Disabled People.* London: Jessica Kingsley.

Burchardt, T. (2000a) The dynamics of being disabled. *Journal of Social Policy* **29** (4) 645–668.

Burchardt, T. (2000b) *Enduring Economic Exclusion: Disabled People, Income and Work.* York: York Publishing Services/Joseph Rowntree Foundation.

Coles, B. (1995) *Youth and Social Policy: Youth Citizenship and Young Careers.* London: UCL Press.

Cooper, J. (2000) *Law, Rights and Disability.* London: Jessica Kingsley.

Dawson, C. (2000) *Independent Successes: Implementing Direct Payments.* York: York Publishing Services/Joseph Rowntree Foundation.

Department for Social Security (1998) *A New Contract for Welfare: Support for Disabled People*, cmd 4103. London: Department for Social Security.

Drake, R. (1999) *Understanding Disability Politics.* London: Macmillan.

Drake, R. (2000) Disabled people, New Labour, benefits and work. *Disability and Society* **20** (4) 421–440.

Glendinning, C. (1983) *Unshared Care: Parents and their Disabled Children.* London: Routledge and Kegan Paul.

Gooding, C. (1996) *Disability Discrimination Act 1995.* London: Blackstone Press.

Gooding, C. (2000) *Disability Discrimination Act:* From statute to practice. *Disability and Society* **20** (4) 533–550.

Gordon, D. & Heslop, P. (1998) Poverty and disabled children. In: D. Dorling and L. Simpson (Eds) *Statistics in Society.* London: Arnold.

Gordon, D., Parker, R., Loughran, F. & Heslop, P. (2000) *Disabled Children in Britain: A Re-analysis of the OPCS Disability Survey.* London: The Stationery Office.

Grove, N., Porter, J. & Morgan, M. (2000) *See What I mean: Guidelines to Aid Understanding of Communication by People with Severe and Profound Learning Disabilities.* Worcestershire: BILD.

Hendey, N. (1998) *Young Adults and Disability: Transition to Independent Living?* PhD thesis, University of Nottingham.

Hirst, M. & Baldwin, S. (1994) *Unequal Opportunities: Growing up Disabled.* London: HMSO.

Hyde, M. (2000) Sheltered and supported employment in the 1990s: The experiences of disabled workers in the UK. *Disability and Society* **13** (2) 199–215.

Jones, G. (1995) *Leaving Home.* Buckingham: Open University Press.

Jones, G. & Bell, R. (2000) *Balancing Acts: Youth, Parenting and Public Policy.* York: Joseph Rowntree Foundation.

Kenworthy, J. & Whittaker, J. (2000) Anything to declare? The struggle for inclusive education and children's rights. *Disability and Society* **15** (2) 219–231.

Kestenbaum, A. (1997) *Disability-Related Costs and Charges for Community Care.* London: DIG.

Kestenbaum, A. (1998) *Work Rest and Pay: The Deal for Personal Assistance Users.* York: York Publishing Services.

Kestenbaum, A. (1999) *What Price Independence?* Bristol: Policy Press/Joseph Rowntree Foundation.

Leicester, M. (1999) *Disability Voice: Towards an Enabling Education.* London: Jessica Kingsley.

Lewis, B. (1993) *Access for Life: A Case for Adaptable, Accessible Homes in a Barrier-Free Environment.* Chesterfield: Derbyshire Coalition of Disabled People.

Millar, J. (2000) *Keeping Track of Welfare Reform: The New Deal Programmes.* York: York Publishing Services.

Morris, J. (1993) *Community Care and Disabled People.* London: Macmillan.

Morris, J. (1997) Care or empowerment? A disability rights perspective. *Social Policy and Administration* **31** (1) 54–60.

Morris, J. (1999a) *Hurtling into a Void: Transition to Adulthood for Young Disabled People with Complex Health and Support Needs.* Brighton: Pavilion.

Morris, J. (1999b) *Move on Up: Supporting Young Disabled People in their Transition to Adulthood.* London: Barnado's.

Morris, J. (2001) Social exclusion and young disabled people with high levels of support needs. *Critical Social Policy* **21** (2) 157–179.

Murray, P. (2000) Disabled children, parents and professionals: Partnership on whose terms? *Disability and Society* **15** (4) 683–698.

Oliver, M. (1996) *Understanding Disability.* London: Macmillan.

Oliver, M. & Barnes, C. (1998) *Disabled People and Social Policy: From Exclusion to Inclusion.* Harlow: Longman.

ONS (2000) *Standard Occupational Classification 2000: Volume I.* London: Office of National Statistics.

Priestley, M. (1999) *Disability Politics and Community Care.* London: Jessica Kingsley.

Priestley, M. (2000) Disability, social policy and the life course. *Journal of Social Policy* **29** (3) 421–439.

Priestley, M. (2001) *Disability and the Life Course.* Cambridge: Cambridge University Press.

Read, J. (2000) *Disability, the Family and Society: Listening to Mothers.* Buckingham: Open University Press.

Riddell, S. (1998)The dynamics of transition to adulthood. In: C. Robinson and K. Stalker (Eds) *Growing Up with Disability.* London: Jessica Kingsley.

Robinson, C. and Stalker, K. (Eds) (1998) *Growing Up with Disability.* London: Jessica Kingsley.

Roulstone, A. (1998) *Enabling Technology: Disabled People, Work and New Technology.* Buckingham: Open University Press.

Social Services Inspectorate (2000) *New Directions for Independent Living: Inspection of Independent Living Arrangements for Younger Disabled People.* London: Department of Health.

Stewart, J., Harris, J. & Sapey, B. (1999) Disability and dependency: Origins and futures of special needs. *Disability and Society* **14** (1) 5–20.

Thomas, C. (1998) Parents and family: Disabled women's stories about their childhood experiences. In: C. Robinson and K. Stalker (Eds) *Growing Up with Disability* pp85–96. London: Jessica Kingsley.

Tisdall, K. (2001) Failing to make the transition? Theorisation of the 'transition to adulthood' for young disabled people. In: M. Priestley (Ed) *Disability and the Life Course.* Cambridge: Cambridge University Press.

Tomlinson, J. (1996) *Inclusive Learning: Report of the Learning Difficulties and/or Disabilities Committee Further Education Funding Council.* London: HMSO.

Ungerson, C. (1997) Social politics and the commodification of care. *Social Politics* **4** (3) 362–381.

Ungerson, C. (1997) Give them the money: Is cash a route to empowerment? *Social Policy and Administration* **31** (1) 45–53.